THE WAY TO GET AN ACCOUNTING JOB IN THE UK

THE 5 STRATEGIC STEPS TO HELP YOU GET AN ACCOUNTING JOB IN 12 WEEKS OR LESS

STERLING LIBS
CHARTERED ACCOUNTANT

Level 33, 25 Canada Square,
Canary Wharf, London E14 5LQ
handbooks@sterlinglibs.com

www.sterlinglibs.com

Editions ISBNs

Softcover		Audio
978-0-9931977-5-8	∎	*978-1-911037-02-6*

i

Success leaves tracks

i. *"Anything is possible, you only need to be clear and specific about what you want and believe you can have it."*
   — Sterling Libs

ii. *"It had long since come to my attention that people of accomplishment rarely sat back and let things happen to them. They went out and happened to things."*
   — Leonardo da Vinci

iii. *"Always bear in mind that your own resolution to succeed is more important than any one thing."*
   — Abraham Lincoln

iv. *"Make a pact with yourself today to not be defined by your past. Sometimes the greatest thing to come out of all your hard work isn't what you get for it, but what you become for it. Shake things up today! Be You...Be Free... Share."*
   — Steve Maraboli, Life, the Truth, and Being Free

Table of Contents

About the author

Sterling Libs FCCA, is a chartered certified accountant, an author and a business consultant.

He runs his own accountancy firm in Canary Wharf London. He also owns a recruitment agency specialising in accounting, finance & IT jobs.

Sterling is so passionate about helping young aspiring accounting professionals to better understand how accounting is done in practice and has been mentoring and training hundreds of graduates and young accounting professionals over the years and many of them have been able to get accounting jobs in the UK and other parts of the world.

He has championed UK practical work experience in accountancy training which has helped many individuals to get accounting jobs in the UK.

Sterling is really gifted in making the seemingly complex simple and throughout his books he shows you fundamental and detailed illustrations with examples of how he does that.

He is really a very inspiring person.

Preface – Note to the reader

The accounting job market like any other job market is a very competitive place mostly due to practical experience requirements and the fact that most employers prefer that you join the team ready to get things going.

You will therefore need to be particularly focussed, determined and resilient in your quest to secure the accounting job of your dreams. It can be tough but it is not an impossible task. There are lots of accounting jobs out there in the market place so don't get discouraged if things seem at first to be hard.

I am going to guide you (hopefully with your cooperation) to your ideal accounting job through the pages of this book. I will be sharing with you fundamental principles, strategies and steps that have helped countless numbers of trainee accountants I have trained and mentored to make the most of their accounting careers.

All that will be required from you is a consistent and passionate commitment to your own success.

I will be showing you how you can systematically and persistently stay on course to getting your ideal accounting job and start earning the money you truly deserve.

I dedicate this to your success and to the glory of God.

Yours truly

Sterling Libs

Warning – Disclaimer

This guide is designed to provide information on how to get an accounting job. It is sold with the understanding that the publisher and author are not engaged in rendering legal, accounting or other professional services. If legal or other expert assistance is required, the services of a competent professional should be sought.

It is not the purpose of this book to reprint all information that is otherwise available on how to find a job, but instead to complement, amplify and supplement other texts. You are urged to read all available material that you can find on this subject and tailor the information to your individual needs.

Succeeding in getting an accounting job will demand a lot from you. Anyone who decides to pursue a career in accounting must expect to invest a lot of time and effort in studying, gaining work experience, looking for a job and maintaining the job.

Every effort has been made to make this book as complete and accurate as possible. However, there may be mistakes, both typographical and in content. Therefore, this text should be used only as a general guide and not as the ultimate source of getting an accounting job.

The purpose of this handbook is to educate and entertain. The author and publisher shall have neither liability nor responsibility to any person or entity with respect to loss or damage caused, or alleged to have been caused, directly or indirectly, by the information contained in this book.

If you do not wish to be bound by the above, you may return this book to the publisher for a full refund before reading any further or using any of the ideas and tips suggested herein.

Introduction

An education in accounting can provide you with entry into a long-term and stable career. There will be a need for accountants of all types as long as there are businesses.

However, getting started in the field can be a challenging prospect. With little to no work experience and few industry connections, figuring out how to find a job in accounting requires taking advantage of all resources available to you.

In this book, I provide you with the resources you can use to systematically and strategically ensure that you succeed in getting an accounting job in 12 weeks or less.

With help, the chances of you finding work are significantly high as successful companies will always need accounting staff to work in their finance departments.

Different sectors and employers all have their own advantages and disadvantages – you have to decide what suits your personality and career aspirations best.

This book will be very invaluable to you as a reference guide while you go about searching, applying, attending job interviews and even managing your first 100 days (famously called your probation period) once you get the job.

Sterling Libs FCCA, London, UK

"If you become immune to the fear of man and deaf to the possibility of failure, success will become your second nature, freedom being your first"

–*Sterling Libs*

The 5 key strategic steps

In my experience, there are 5 key things that you can do to give yourself a winning chance of securing an accounting job as you navigate the job market.

These five things are:

1. *Time usage assessment & planning*
2. *Getting practical work experience*
3. *Having a mentor*
4. *CV preparation and presentation*
5. *Marketing yourself successfully.*

Let's look at each of them in a bit more detail. Shall we?

Turn over please.

1. Time usage assessment & planning:

"If you can't manage time well, you can't manage wealth" - **Sterling Libs**.

If you want to succeed in getting an accounting job faster, then I suggest you start by looking at how you are currently spending your time.

I don't need to explain this to you but I am hopping you know that there is nothing worthwhile you will ever accomplish without time. Time is indispensable to any endeavour and any success in anything including finding yourself an accounting job.

You simply can't afford to waste time, not when you are serious about your life and career. Benjamin Franklin said in one of his books *"if thou would love life, do not squander time, for that is the stuff that life is made of"*. Mmmm, wise words, worth paying attention to.

Succeeding in getting your ideal accounting job is not going to be about working and searching for jobs for long hours each day, no, not that, it's more about getting more done in the hours you devote to your accountancy career job strategy.

How you spend your time is entirely up to you, it is your time after all, but make no mistake; misuse of your time will cost you big. That is a guarantee.

In this book, I have for your benefit a time usage assessment & planner form which I personally use to be effective in my time usage and I have also used it to help some of my diligent trainees and the results are simply awesome. It is very effective in helping you use your time strategically in accomplishing your goals.

It is very simple to use and I've found it very remarkable. You just need to be clear and specific about what you want and the sky will be your limit.

When using this time usage assessment and planner form (there is a blank copy at appendix 1 at the end of this book or you can download a copy by visiting www.sterlinglibs.co.uk and clicking on help sheets), I recommend that you begin by doing an assessment of your current reality in terms of how you are using your time. Make a note of everything you habitually do on a daily basis and find out how much time you take doing each of those things.

You should then, make readjustments on your time and draw up a new time plan taking into account your ideal accounting job as a major goal that you should devote most of your time to. Make it a point that until you get that job most of your time should be spent on things and strategies that will get you closer and closer to it every day.

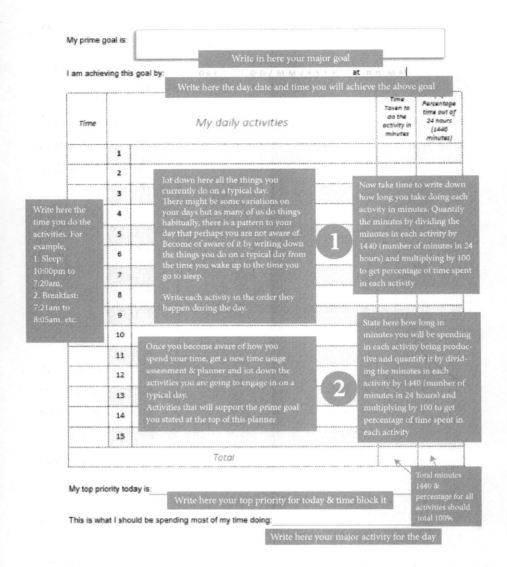

This is the current time usage assessment exercise. You are basically finding out how you are currently using your time

This is a purposeful time usage planning exercise. You are basically reordering your priorities and what you choose to spend your time doing in a more conscious manner in light of your prime goal

2. Getting practical work experience

The second strategy is quite obvious but non the less bears m᷉ about getting or having relevant practical work experience.

You will soon realise (if you haven't yet) that the accounting job market in the UK is so competitive that only those with requisite practical experience stand a better chance of moving faster and securing accounting roles than those without.

So, if you don't have sufficient practical work experience, get some.

You can get practical work experience in various ways: volunteering, internships or practical hands on work experience training like one provided by TD&A Certified Accountants (www.tdanda.co.uk/careers) and various other firms.

If you are still studying, please do not wait until you finish your studies to start getting work experience. Take some time and get practical work experience in accountancy while still studying. You will be doing yourself a very big favour. If you want to get some practical work experience in accountancy, I recommend TD&A certified accountants - see their web address above.

I recommend TD&A certified accountants because their work experience fits around your schedules, you enroll at anytime and progress at your own pace with expert guidance and mentoring given on a one-to-one basis. The work experience is hands-on (100% practical, not theory) by qualified and experienced accountants and they will start you off from scratch and build your experience step by step in a systematic and professional manner.

5. Having a mentor

The other aspect of your job success strategy will involve having a mentor.

Mentoring is when one individual actively and willingly passes his/her knowledge and wisdom onto another person. It is one of the oldest forms of influence and knowledge sharing. It started with the ancient Greeks; mentor was Odysseus' trusted counsellor and advisor. He/she is an individual—usually older, but always more experienced, who helps and guides another individual's development.

This guidance is done without the expectation of personal or monetary gain on the mentor's part.

Mentors can be friends, relatives, co-workers, teachers, supervisors, etc. There is no official title.

It is very important as you embark on this journey of securing your ideal accounting job that you enlist the help and guidance of a mentor and make sure that you align your goals with their expertise and experience.

It is also very important for you to remember that when you find a mentor, he/she will be doing it from the goodness of his/her heart, so being a good protégée (someone being mentored) is the best way to ensure the relationship enjoys a healthy purposeful existence. You as a protégéé need to be:

- *Committed to expanding your capabilities and focused on achieving professional results.*

- *Willing to ask for help.*

- *Open and receptive to learning and trying new ideas.*

- *Able to accept feedback—even constructive criticism—and act upon it.*

- *Willing to experiment and apply what you learn back on the job search or even in your job once you get one.*

- *Able to communicate and work cooperatively with others.*

- *Be personally responsible and accountable.*

- *Ready, willing and able to meet on a regular basis.*

The key to having a successful mentor protégée relationship is for you and your mentor to be clear about what the relationship is going to look like and how it will be managed. You should discuss things like:

- *Contact and response times*

- *Meetings*

- *Confidentiality*

- *Focus*

- *Feedback*

- *Goals and accountability*

I will provide you with some ideas and ways of securing for yourself one such an advisor and counsellor because I believe a good mentor is very invaluable to your accounting career and generally success in life.

So, here are three things you can do get yourself a mentor.

i. Identify the target

What is your ultimate career destination in the accounting profession? Is it to become a Finance director of a FTSE 100 company, is it to become a tax consultant, is it to become a finance manager? What is it? You have to be absolutely clear about this.

ii. Select your mentor candidate

You should then think about someone who is exceptionally experienced or talented in the area you have chosen as your ultimate accounting career job, it could be someone you know personally, or it could be a leader in the accounting profession or perhaps someone who is recognised as a top authority in the area of accounting you want to specialise in. Whoever it is, it is your responsibility to make sure he or she has a proven track record and is truly successful. Get at least ten of them – ten names.

Once you have done your bit here, you should then,

iii. Create a strategic plan to contact them

Here, the most important thing is to be sincere, it does go a long way in helping you get what you want in life.

When making first contact with your researched mentor to be, get right to the point. Busy people (of which your proposed mentor is more likely to be) appreciate this. Don't socialise. Stick to a well–prepared script using conversational tone. For example, say something like:

"Hello Mr/Ms (name), my name is Frank. We haven't met yet and I know you are a busy person, so I'll be brief. I am a recent graduate/student in Accounting and Finance. Over the years, you have done a fantastic job, building your professional accounting career. I am sure you had some real challenges when you were first starting out.

Well, I am still in those early stages, trying to figure everything out on how to eventually become as successful as you are. Mr/Ms (Name), I would really appreciate it if you would consider being my mentor. All that would mean is spending 10 minutes on the phone with me once a month and 30 minutes face to face meeting once every month, so I could ask you a few questions and learn from you.

I would really appreciate it. Would you be open to that?"

Here is the point; it is important that you control the conversation in the initial contact. Say what you want to say, ask the closing question and then shut up.

When you ask that closing question – "Would you be open to that?" the answer will usually be "Yes" or "No". If it's "Yes", control your excitement and ask a follow-up question - "When would be a good time to call you in the next few weeks?"

Confirm the specific time for your first call and meeting and send a thank note to him/her right away.

If it's a "No", well, contact the next person in the list of potential mentors you researched until one says "Yes", you simply have to persist. One of them will say "Yes".

Remember, before you make the first call, it's useful to have as much information as possible from your search about your potential mentor as far as his professional achievements are concerned and any projects he or she has been involved or is involved in.

All the best to you, I am sure you will get that mentor. A mentor is a critical component of your job success. Get yourself one, do whatever it takes.

Right, so far, we have looked at three of the five things that can help you navigate the job market with a much more assured sense of success, they are;

- *time usage assessment & planning*

- *getting practical work experience*

- *getting yourself a mentor*

The fourth aspect of your accounting job success strategy is: CV preparation & presentation.

4. CV preparation and presentation

We will now turn our attention to the fourth aspect of your accounting job success strategy and it is all about how to avoid being rejected for any accounting job you apply for. The things we will be looking at include the following;

    i.   *Writing an eye catching CV*

    ii.   *Researching employers*

    iii. *Presenting your CV*

    iv. *Writing professional cover letters*

Let's look at each of them in turn.

i. How to write an eye catching CV

Your CV plays a very important part in your job success strategy.

So, let me mention a few remarks about CV's and I give this remarks firstly as an employer and secondly as somebody who also owns & runs a recruitment agency helping connect candidates and employers in Accountancy, Finance and IT.

Here are my remarks:

There is a common misconception that a CV is just a list of job duties and responsibilities you've performed in the past. This in my opinion is what keeps most people from creating a CV that really highlights their skills and their talents - what I call an eye catching & winning CV.

So what exactly is a CV?

Well, your CV should be an advertising and marketing campaign document/copy designed to sell one thing - YOU. And since your CV is part of your advertising and marketing campaign, creating a CV is much more involved than simply writing down your education and your work history.

You can use the same strategies that advertising firms use in their campaigns to advertise and market yourself.

The starting point is to know clearly and specifically what accounting job you want. Make that your point of focus.

Once you know exactly what it is that you want, you'll then begin conducting research to know which employers meet your goals. From this research, you'll write down the top ten employers you would like to work for and begin focusing on your number one on down.

Then you'll figure out what the employer is looking for by continuing your research. All of this research will help you target each CV that you send by matching the needs of the employer with your transferable skills and your experience. We will talk a bit more about researching employers later.

When writing your CV, keep in mind that the idea is to promote your largest personal investment, YOU. Tell them what you could do for them and how you will be an asset to their business. And don't think of it as bragging. You're simply showing employers what they will get if they hire you and how you can make a difference in their company.

There is a simple technique to create a CV that showcases the experience that you bring to the table in the best possible light. This technique helps you show off your accomplishments and your achievements, demonstrating what you can offer, and how you will be an asset to the company overall.

The technique is famously called the "PAR formula"

PAR stands for Problem-Action-Result. The PAR formula tells a business story. In the case of your CV, you can use this formula to tell your success story to potential employers, the story that will show how you can help them and why you are the perfect candidate for the job.

All good stories have one thing in common, a beginning, middle, and end.

The PAR formula works the same way. The beginning is the problem, the middle is the action, and the end is the result. During your career, you probably had problems, you did take action to solve those problems, and hopefully received positive end results. Your CV should not be a laundry list of boring job duties, and responsibilities that you've performed.

You'll get much greater results by using PAR formula to showcase how you will help your prospective employer with their bottom line. As an added bonus, creating PAR statements can even help prepare you for behaviour-based interview questions, such as 'what do you consider to be your greatest achievement?'

So how does it work?

Let me begin by giving you a few examples. Let's say that you worked previously in a role as a trainee accountant or sales ledger clerk. The problem that you may have had in this role was a lot of bad debts and very law working capital for the organisation.

What action did you take? Well, you had a meeting with your supervisor, consulted all the clients in default of payments to understand what the issues were and based on your findings, you designed an effective way to collect the outstanding's while still ensuring that the clients don't leave the business and even ensured that over 90% of them got into the direct debit/

standing order system of paying future purchases from the organisation – something that your predecessors in this role were not able to do before you.

The result was a significant reduction in bad debts by over 80% and an increase in cash flow and working capital and less borrowings and interest rates payments as well as increased efficiency in the sales ledger department as less time was now spent in chasing debts since many of the clients were now on direct debit.

Doesn't that sound better than simply saying "collecting outstanding debts from debtors and doing various other aspects of sales ledger?"

Now, let's take a look at what PAR statement would look like if you were an administrative assistant.

The problem was that the company was using an antiquated Jingalong system for their contact management system. The action that you took was that you created a new contact management database using Access (because you have very good Microsoft office skills).

Your result was that the company can now use the information from the database to merge addresses for mass mailings and electronic mail distribution, saving time and money. This also increased efficiency, shortening the time it takes to send out mass mailings by over 85%.

The PAR statement for this example would be, 'created a contact management system using Access to store data from outdated Jingalong systems, increasing efficiency of mass mailings to our clients by 90%'.

Doesn't this sound better than 'sent out letters to clients'? Both of these examples contain action verbs and details.

They also use numbers to quantify the results of the action. It sets your experience in motion.

So, how do you write your own PAR statements?

Always start at the beginning, the problem. What are some of the biggest problems that you faced in your career, the action that you took to resolve the problem, and the positive outcome that ensued as a result of your actions?

Think of things you've done in your career/training that you're proud of. Show the employer that you can take action when the situation arises. And don't let PAR statements intimidate you. It's not rocket science. It's easy. Have fun with it!

If you're still stuck, try answering questions such as, did you win any awards? Did you direct, oversee, or manage any projects? Did you implement any new ideas? Did you organise an event or a function? Did you save the company time, money, or make something on the job more efficient? It can even be something such as getting promoted quickly.

For example, you could say, promoted from bookkeeper to assistant accountant within eight months of your initial hiring. Think back, think hard, and have some fun creating your own PAR statements.

So, there you have it, make an excellent PAR statement and you will sure be leap frogging your peers in the race to the accounting jobs.

The basic principle is this: every CV you send out should be customised and tailored to meet the needs of each prospective employer. Items on your CV that are unrelated or irrelevant to the targeted position should be downplayed or removed. Related accomplishments and achievements should be highlighted, as should your transferable skills, throughout each and every position you've held.

Targeting your CV for each desired position allows you to emphasise how you are the perfect match for that particular job.

Okay, that said, let us now look at the next aspect

ii. Researching employers

In this section, we will be attempting to answer the following questions;

- *Who do you want to work for?*

- *Where would you best fit in?*

- *Do you want to work for a small company that is family-oriented, or perhaps a huge corporation with plenty of upward mobility?*

Once you know what you want, it's time to begin your homework. Always keep in mind that your CV is your advertising campaign document. Advertising executives always begin a campaign with market research.

So how and where do you begin from?

Write down the top then employers you would like to work for. Then focus your marketing campaign by conducting research on your number one on down. After you've decided who you want to target, find out as much information as possible. Researching the employer will help you to better target your CV by knowing the employer's needs. The closer you can match your skills and achievements to their needs, the better your results will be. It will also help you during the interview to show the employer you're interested enough in their company to find out all you can about them.

One of the best research tools at your disposal is using the Internet. Begin by locating their website using a search engine like Google or Yahoo! Let's say that you want to work for ABN Europe. Once you've located their web site, look for section such as About Us.

You may also look for information such as history and careers and their eam, find out who their CEO is, etc.

...ote of the company's mission statement and consider trying to incorporate your own version of it into your cover letter and your CV.

Next, find out what the organisational structure is like: whether it's a privately or a publicly held company. If the company you're looking at is publicly held, you've got a few more options for research. Look them up on the London stock exchange or the NASDAQ especially for US based listed companies.

You can research public employers on the London stock exchange and/or the New York Stock Exchange. It is the world's largest stock exchange by market capitalisation.

If the company you are looking to work for is based in the USA, you can research SEC filings to find out more about the company's financial health. SEC stands for Securities and Exchange Commission. Check out employers on the Hoovers web site. Hoovers includes an extensive database that gives insight and analysis about companies, organisations, and industries.

See if you can find anything about the company through all the sources available

Research statistical information in your industry, such as projections, trends, and layoff information. Check out newspaper articles, trade journals, and business magazines.

What other information should you look for?

Who are their competitors? That would be good information to have at hand

Research the market and find out all about their competition. What are their products and their services? How many years have they been in business? How many employees and locations do they have? Are they a subsidiary or a parent company?

The point to remember here is this; when beginning your job search, you must know what you want first and which employers will be your best fit. One size does not fit all. Then you must know what the employer wants.

Remember, each CV should be targeted towards a particular employer and job description.

The more you know about the employer and their wants and needs, the better you'll be able to match your skills to those needs. And the more you know about the company, the better you will be able to do during your interview by appearing more knowledgeable.

By doing your homework, you'll leave a positive impression with the employer and stand out from the crowd. You'll be prepared to answer any questions they may have and will be in a better position to create an excellent eye catching CV.

So how do you go about presenting your CV once you have prepared it?

Let's have a look at it, shall we?

iii. Presenting your CV professionally

Printing, copying, and the importance of paper.

I'll let you in on a secret.

In the real world, most especially the professional world, stay professional throughout your job search. You have done all of this hard work so far to make the contents of your CV perfect. The home stretch is not the place to slow down. Believe it or not, even the paper you use is part of your marketing campaign.

Before a potential employer can read your CV, they must visually see your CV and then physically touch and feel the paper.

Even if you're not snail mailing or sending it by post, you will be giving them a physical copy during the interview. Both of these senses can make a good or a bad impression on your audience. If the employer sees a CV that is visually appealing, it will entice them to pick it up. After picking it up, they can either feel cheap copy paper or a sophisticated and classier cotton fibre bond or linen blend. Go to any office supply store and invest in buying CV paper.

You can also order off the Internet as well. As far as colours go, stay away from anything florescent. Stick with a light professional-looking colour such as cream, white, beige, or a light grey.

Whatever you pick, just make sure it looks professional. Most CV papers are a bit heavier than the standard paper. For example, standard is 80 GSM, while CV paper is a little thicker, about 120 GSM. It is much more durable, feels better to the touch, and has a much more polished look.

Next, make sure you use a laser printer as opposed to inkjet. You would be very surprised at the difference between a CV printed on an inkjet printer and a CV printed from a laser, most especially when printed on the cotton fibre and linen blends.

I encourage you not to stop before you get to the finish line by putting your masterpiece in the wrong canvas and buying a cheap frame so to say. Consider the type of paper you purchase as part of your marketing campaign. By purchasing quality, professional paper and using the best printer available, you will appeal to both the employer's sense of sight and touch, even if they don't realise it's happening.

Did you know that there are more nerve endings in a person's fingertips than just about any other part of the body; therefore, utilising quality paper will make them feel, quite literally, that you are a person of quality. That is the sort of impression you should be conveying.

Using a high-quality printer will let them see clearly that you are the professional quality.

One more thing, when sending your CV by post/snail mail, don't forget to put it in a do not bend envelop and send it by recorded delivery or signed for postage method.

Now let's look at another crucial aspect CV preparation & presentation.

iv. How to write professional cover letters

Never send a CV alone when applying for a job. Whether you hear about the job opening from a friend, read about it in the newspaper or a magazine, or find it in any job listings, learn as much as you can about the employer and the job and use this information to develop your cover letters.

Letters are personal communications from you to another individual. Your letters should have absolutely no errors: no typos, no misspelled words and no noticeable corrections.

Each letter you write should be short, fitting easily on one page with generous margins on all sides. Paragraphs should be limited to four to six lines whenever possible, because business letters are usually scanned quickly. The first line of each paragraph is most important and the last line is second most important.

As you work on drafts of letters, try reading only the first lines of each paragraph to see what information is communicated.

Your name and address should be typed on the letter. Standard business form, with your address and the date at the top right, the addressee's name and address at the left just above the salutation, is preferable. At the end of the letter, your full name should be typed below your signature.

Letters should be addressed to an individual by name, with correct title and address. In most correspondence the salutation will be "Dear Mr. Jones", "Dear Ms. Jenkins". First names should not be used unless you are personally acquainted with the addressee. It is advisable to try to find out whether a woman prefers to be addressed as "Miss", "Mrs" or "Ms", but if her preference is not known, "Ms." is acceptable.

There are two kinds of letters you will be writing during your job search: letters applying for a job (cover letters), and follow-up letters.

Cover letters

The objective of the cover letter is to impress the employer with your qualifications, motivation and interest in the job so that he will want to interview you. The first paragraph should identify clearly what job you are applying for and why you are interested in the job. If a mutual friend recommended that you apply for the job, mention their name.

In the appendix 2 at the end of this manual, I have two descriptions and samples of cover letters, which I hope will be helpful suggestions and models. Personalise them because your letters should be personal communications to the individual you are addressing, saying what you want to say as clearly and directly as possible.

Follow-up letters

In follow-up letters your objective is to say thank you, to express interest in a continuing relationship, and to structure the next step.

Okie dokie, let's move on.

Now, let's look at the fifth aspect of success to deploy in our 5 step strategic plan. *It is all about presence.*

5. Marketing yourself successfully

In this section we are going to look at how you can increase your visibility to employers & recruitment consultants and how to write thank you notes as part of your marketing strategy.

If you are not visible or easily locatable by employers and recruitment agencies, then it is almost like you don't exist as far as they are concerned.

While job searching, make it very obvious & easy for employers & recruitment consultants to find you.

The two effective ways I know of doing so is by using key words on your CV to make your CV easily searchable on the internet and secondly, by having a professional online presence.

Let's talk about each of them beginning with:

a. Having key words on your CV

One of the most important and essential steps in creating your CV is incorporating the use of keywords.

You see, recruiters search for potential employees the same way you use Google to search for a topic, that is, with one or more words. But instead of using Google, they use an applicant tracking system, or ATS for short, which quickly scans for words matching their criteria.

If the keywords in your CV match the criteria they typed in, wala! You have now won the first round by simply being found. If those keywords are not found, neither are you. Do you get the point?

Therefore, it is absolutely crucial to incorporate these keywords throughout your CV to maximise your chances of being found in a sea of hundreds of

negative information out there, but don't worry. Most recruiters do keep this in mind, especially when you have a more common name.

If someone writes some unfavourable information on your wall or social network pages, delete the information if you have the option to (which I think is available on most social networking sites), but remember, a recruiter may see it even before you do.

You may choose to use the options and settings available in Facebook and other social networks to hide your page from those outside your social network. At least when seeking employment, this is usually a good option to set. Most employers and recruiters nowadays are computer savvy enough to know how to find you on Facebook, Myspace, and other social networking pages during their research.

I have heard of a case where one recruiter said that a position was actually offered to a candidate and then rescinded because the recruiter had found very negative and detrimental information on their Facebook page after the fact. The candidate lost the opportunity of being hired.

The moral here is that; be careful and cautious of what you write, post, blog, broadcast, and upload. Also be cautious of what you place on sites such as YouTube.

LinkedIn, on the other hand, is a better choice as a professional networking resource. You should use LinkedIn for your professional page only. Don't make it your social network page and of course, remember keep it very professional.

The bottom line here is that you need to be visible to employers and recruiters for you to even stand a chance of being seen. The two key ways you can increase and enhance your visibility is by using key words on your CV and also by creating a professional online personification and image. Do remember however to keep your online personification & image clean to avoid your dream job being rescinded simply because the hiring manager or recruitment consultant saw something negative about you on the Internet.

c. Writing thank-you notes

Let me share with you some sobering truth; did you know that a majority of people that attend interviews fail to send a thank-you note afterward?

Now, let me tell you a secret, when you send yours (thank you note), you'll stand out from the crowd as being thoughtful and courteous, someone that respects the time that others took out of their busy schedules to meet with you. It also gives you a chance to reinforce your qualifications for the position.

Do yourself a favour, send a thank-you note or email no more than 24 hours after your interview.

And remember, to send your thank-you note to each person you interviewed with. Try to get a business card from each person you meet with and send each a separate note. This way you'll have the correct spelling of their name, their correct title, their address, the phone number, and email, when you're writing your thank-you notes.

Each note should be a separate thank-you written towards each person, not a carbon copy. For example, perhaps you had a panel interview and you met with the HR Director, three would-be co-workers and one would-be boss. Send each a different thank-you note. Don't forget to also send thank-you notes to each of your references and mentor(s). They took the time out of their busy schedules to help you out.

Take the time out of your busy schedule to thank them properly. Also, consider sending thank-you notes to anyone that gave you a lead or has assisted you in any way along your job-search journey.

Just remember when writing thank-you notes not to copy line for line from a book or something you found on the Internet. Be professional, polite, and let your own personality shine through

Let's look at a few suggestions on what to include.

First of all, thank them for taking the time to meet with you. Convey excitement and interest in the position and thank them for the information you received during the interview. Reiterate your top qualifications for the job. Try to include unique things that make you the perfect candidate for the position. Align yourself with the expectations of the employer for this particular position by highlighting a couple of the things the interviewers singled out as the most important to perform this specific job and how you can outperform those expectations.

Add any additional information you may have forgotten to mention during the interview. Give them your contact information once again. Be sure to include your email and mobile phone number. Conclude with the sentence such as, "Thank you for your time and consideration." Use "Respectfully" or "Sincerely" as you are closing.

Close by saying, "I'll look forward to hearing from you soon" after giving them your contact information.

If the company or interviewer is more traditional, you should send via post. On the other hand, if all of your correspondence thus far has been using electronic means, then you may continue in this vein.

Sending a thank-you note may just well be your centre in getting the job.

It shows you have proper etiquette and manners. It can be yet another way of restating your qualifications, and it puts you in front of the interviewer once again. Since there are so many others that are no longer showing his respect for the employer's time and consideration, it is yet another way of making you and your qualifications stand out from the crowd.

Don't miss this important step in clinching the deal by showing your esteem and respect for the employer, your excitement about the job, and how your top qualifications make you the best candidate for the position.

Making it all happen - finally getting that job

The job success action planner

The job success action planner is meant to help you focus all that we have talked about in the preceding sections in utilising your time and resources to secure that ideal accounting job. It is more about being clear about what you want & making up your mind to go for it. It is also about taking 100% responsibility for that next level of your accounting career.

Having gone through a lot of useful and strategic stuff in the preceding sections, now is the time to put all of it together to work for you.

It is time to take ACTION!

Let me say this quite bluntly (forgive me if it will hurt your feelings, I don't mean to), your accounting career success is your responsibility and if you don't take that responsibility seriously, it is you who is going to lose out. If you are not serious about your own success, don't expect anyone else to be. You cannot shank or delegate this responsibility to anyone, it is squarely yours and you must do whatever you can to make a positive difference in your own life.

That said, when you choose to focus your time and energy to finding an accounting job, you are most likely to geometrically increase your chances of succeeding in securing that job.

I have designed here for you an action planner for this purpose.

Each of the sections of the action planner are explained in the figure in the next page and I urge you to carefully study it and diligently use it every week over the course of 12 weeks.

If you diligently use this action planner (see illustration in the next page) and heed to the advice and instructions in the preceding sections, I have no doubt in my mind that you will get that accounting job in 12 weeks or less. You can find a blank copy in appendix 1 towards the end of this book or by visiting my website at www.sterlinglibs.co.uk and clicking on help sheets

Here is what Denis Waitley, Albert Einstein once said:

"A sign of wisdom and maturity is when you come to terms with the realisation that your decisions cause your rewards and consequences. You are responsible for your life, and your ultimate success depends on the choices you make."
Denis Waitley

"Man must cease attributing his problems to his environment, and learn again to exercise his will – his personal responsibility."
Albert Einstein

"When you blame others, you give up your power to change."
Unknown

I differ the last word in this section to Jesus Christ. Here is what He said:

"If you can believe, all things are possible to him who believes" Mark 9:23
Jesus Christ

JOB SUCCESS ACTION PLANNER

Name: *Write your name here*

Week commencing: *Write here the start day of the week*

My ideal job title: *Write your ideal job title here*

Proposed Start date: D D/ M M/ Y Y Y Y *Write ideal job start date here*

Top 3 goals for this week

1

2   *Here, you list your top 3 goals for the week & prioritise them*

3

Date this week to achieve the goals

D D/ M M/ Y Y Y Y

D   *The deadline for achieving each of the 3 goals should be written here*

D

No.	Things to do this week	Mon	Tues	Wed	Thurs	Fri	Sat	Sun	Goal	Achived
1	Search & apply for jobs									
2	Read: Psycho-cybernetics by Maxwell Maltz for 15 minutes									
3	Phone call/meeting with mentor									
4	Meeting with a successful person									
5	Direct call/contact with employers									
6										
7										
8										
9										
10										

In this section, if for example, you plan to search & apply for 3 jobs each day this week – Mon to Sun (3 jobs x7 days =21 times).

Write this number (21) down on the goals section for search & apply for jobs.

Now, during the week, record on each day (Mon, Tue, Wed ......) how many times you actually searched and applied for jobs, add up the times and multiply by number of days in the week you searched and applied for jobs and put the result on the Achieved section for search & apply for jobs.

Repeat this exercise for each and every activity for the week listed on the left.

From 6 – 10, write your own activities that you will do to help you get a job. Perhaps something like: go for networking events etc.

Successful people I am meeting this week

No	Name	Day	Time
1			
2			
3			

Make it a point to meet at least 3 successful persons each week. Write the names of the ones you are meeting this week here and the time (day & time) you are meeting them

Job interviews booked for next week

No.	Agency/employer	date	Time
1			
2			
3			

Moments of reflection

What are you grateful for this week: *Write in here at least one thing you give thanks for: any good thing that happened to you or somebody else you know.*

If you were to start this week all over again, what one thing would you do differently:

Write here a note of what you would do differently to help you achieve your goals for the week faster, and effortlessly if you had a fresh start. Try to implement what you would do differently in the coming week

Jobs you can apply for in Accounting

Hope you have familiarised yourself with the job success action planner and are already using it as one of your strategic job planning tools.

Here are the most common jobs in accounting that you could potentially apply for.

i. Bookkeeper

Job profile: Most of the time you'll work 9am to 5pm, Monday to Friday. There may be the odd times when it's really quite busy (like during yearend) and you need to work a few extra hours.

Your main role is to maintain financial records for the company and to do your job effectively, you ought to have a detail-oriented approach to work that will allow you to keep up with company expenditures, income, and payroll as well as tax requirements.

There are positions across a wide range of organisations, so it's up to you to choose an industry you are interested in - health, public sector, private sector, charities etc.

There are opportunities for part-time and job sharing. Temporary work is often available too. You could also work freelance to work the hours that suit you.

The larger the company you work for, the more opportunities for progression there will be.

Salary: For a new starter you can expect to earn between £12,000 and £14,000 a year. As you get more experience you'll be able to earn up to £20,000. On average, for an experienced and qualified bookkeeper salary can be £23,000-£27,500 (Association for Accounting Technicians)

ii. Sales Ledger clerk

Job profile: Sales ledger clerks form the administrative side of an accounting team. You'll spend most of your time at your desk raising invoices and talking to clients.

This job is ideal for you if you want a career that offers room to move as there's plenty of scope for promotion once you've got some experience. Sales ledger clerks often graduate to work as a supervisor or manager and from there to credit controller and even financial controller.

Your main duties will include:

- *Setting up new clients*
- *Producing invoices*
- *Sorting out any rebates, posts and filing*
- *Running off turnover statements*
- *Banking and reconciliation*
- *Checking sales VAT has been included on invoices*
- *Chasing up outstanding debts*

Salary: Starting salary can be around £18,000 to £20,000. This will increase to £30,000 plus once you take on a more supervisory role.

iii. Purchase ledger clerk

Job profile: Typical work hours are 9:00am – 5:00pm Monday to Friday. Your responsibilities will depend on the size of the company you work for, and you may have sole control over payments or work as part of a much bigger purchase ledger team. Purchase ledger clerks are expected to be able to:

- *Code and check supplier invoices*

- *Work out VAT payments*

- *Check and reconcile supplier statements*

- *Pay out money via BACS or by cheque*

- *Deal with purchase enquiries*

- *File invoices and statements*

- *Process staff expenses*

- *Manage petty cash*

Salary: As a starter, you should expect your salary to range from £16,000-£23,000 per year, depending on your experience and qualifications.

iv. Accounts Assistant

Job profile: As an Accounts assistant you will provide administrative support to accountants, handling mail and basic bookkeeping and undertaking clerical tasks such as making phone calls, typing, and filing

Depending on the size of the organisation you work for, the tasks you will be performing include but not limited to:

- *Assisting with all aspects of sales & purchase ledger*

- *Assisting with the preparation of statutory accounts.*
- *Assisting with credit control and debtor management.*
- *Calculating and checking to make sure payments, amounts and records are correct.*
- *Working with spreadsheets and journals.*
- *Sorting out incoming and outgoing daily post and answering any queries.*
- *Managing petty cash transactions.*
- *Reconciling finance accounts and direct debits.*
- *Assisting with payroll and posting payroll journals*

Salary: Accounts assistants earn an average of £18,500 – £22,000 a year (for full-time hours), but the starting salary can be as little as £13, 000 for inexperienced employees.

v. Credit Controller

Job profile: This is primarily an office-based role where you'll be expected to work 9:00am -5:00pm, Monday to Friday with some overtime at busy periods such as the end of the year. The beauty of this role is that credit control principles are the same whatever industry you work in and you can move into different sectors. With enough experience you could even become the go to person – consultant.

It will be your responsibility to review debt recovery procedures and stop the supply of goods and services - or even start the serious process of legal action - if a client has paid late or missed multiple payments. It's not the nicest part of the job, but someone's got to do it. You may be required to attend meetings with clients or occasionally court hearings if you're taking legal action against a client.

Generally, your role will include performing the following tasks:

- *Ensuring customers pay on time*

- *Setting up the terms and conditions of credit to customers*

- *Deciding whether or not to offer the credit and how much to offer to a client*

- *Checking customer's credit ratings with banks*

- *Negotiating re-payment plans*

- *Dealing with internal queries about payments*

Salary: The starting salary for a credit controller can range between £17,000 and £28,000 per year but this can rise to over £45,000 plus if you move up the ladder to become a credit control manager.

vi. Tax Adviser

Job profile: As a tax adviser you will provide a professional advisory and consultancy service to clients, interpret complicated tax legislation (and it's implications to the client) and plan the best strategy to plan clients financial affairs and minimise future tax liabilities.

You could work for an accountancy firm, a specialist tax consultancy or a company with its own tax team. Banks, legal firms and HM Revenue and Customs also need good tax specialists.

You could also choose to become a freelance tax consultant and start your own business. Why not?

The typical duties to perform in this role will include but not limited to:

- *Researching and understanding tax law*

- *Liaising with HM Revenue and Customs on your clients' behalf*

- *Checking and completing tax forms*

- *Meeting clients to gather information and explain options available to them*

- *Auditing clients' tax records*

Individuals, small businesses and large companies all need good, clear and simple tax advice. So your job is really a very important one and one you should cherish.

Salary: Starting at £20,000-£37,000 rising to £30,000-£55,000 upon obtaining the ATT qualification (ATT) or even £65,000 plus with the CTA qualification and substantial experience.

vii. Payroll Administrator

Job profile: You'll be involved with creating new payroll policies and procedures, reporting back to the management team and ensuring all the computer systems are up to date in terms of government legislation like RTI, pensions etc.

As part of the payroll administration team the duties that you will perform include but are not limited to the following:

- *Checking people's hours*

- *Making the weekly or monthly salary/wage payments on time*

- *Issuing payslips to employees*

- *Working out tax and national insurance deductions*

- *Submitting the payroll report to HMRC*

- *Providing the accountants with the payroll journal figures to be posted into the accounts*

- *Setting up new members of staff on the payroll*

- *Calculating overtime*

- *Issuing tax forms (P45s, P60, etc.)*

- *Managing special situations like maternity or sickness, holiday*

You could work as part of the payroll team in an organisation or for a payroll bureau - a company that specialises in running the payroll for other companies.

Average salary: If you're just starting out as a payroll administrator you should be on £13,000 to £18,000 a year. This jumps up to £20,000 and £25,000 as you get more qualified and more experienced.

viii. Finance Manager

Job profile: As a finance manager you'll work with all departments of the business to help them plan and manage their budgets. You'll also work closely with the CEO to help him/her manage the overall business so it makes the most money it can.

Where you work will have an impact on the work you do. In a bigger company the role is often more strategic and involves a lot of analysis and you might be the finance director for a division rather than for the whole company. If you work for a smaller company you'll probably have to be a bit more hands on with general accounts matters too.

It's a broad and interesting role covering activities like:

- *Monitoring cash flow*

- *Supervising your own accounts team*

- *Monitoring business performance*

- *Developing financial models*

- *Preparing accounts*

- *Overseeing the budgets and that everyone is sticking to them*

- *Working with departments and teams*

- *Planning for the future*

- *Competitor analysis*

- *Strategic planning*

Average salary: £53,660 (GMB/ONS)

ix. Management Accountant

Job profile: Management accountants look to the future rather than the past when assessing the financial status of an organisation. Their role is to provide the financial information necessary to enable an organisation's management team to make sound strategic decisions.

Some organisations will have their own management accountants. You could also work for a private accountancy firm which offers accountancy services to fee-paying clients.

The kind of activities you'll oversee include:

- *Making sure spending is in line with budgets*

- *Recommending ways of cutting costs*

- *Analysing your company's financial performance and making longer term forecasts*

- *Providing information for audits*

- *Working with all departments and the management team to help make financial decisions*

A big focus of your job will be to make sure the business is compliant with financial governance requirements.

You'll most likely manage a team who will help you with all your duties although the role does vary quite widely depending on the size of the business and what sector it is in.

Average salary: Typical starting salary is £21,000, £30,000-£45,000 with experience rising to £60,000+ for senior position (CIMA)

x. Auditor

Job profile: As an auditor your job is to ensure that an organisation is using its resources in the most efficient ways – whether for the sake of the taxpayer in the public sector, or shareholders in private businesses.

You are responsible for auditing the accounts of an organisation, analysing expenditure and its effectiveness, assessing risks to financial control and accountability.

You'll not only have to write reports on your findings, but you may also find yourself in a boardroom giving PowerPoint presentations to managers and directors. You'll be expected to keep on top of the many changes in the law and keep a rational view of the best way ahead when all around you people are flapping in a panic.

You will in many instances need strong communication skills, lots of tact, and confidence in your own ability.

Average salary: On a graduate trainee scheme straight out of college, your starting salary will be £18,000-£22,000 a year. Once you're fully-fledged, an auditor can expect to earn £35,000-£45,000 in a public sector position, rising to well over £60,000 as a senior audit manager. £49,072 - £63,235 is the average according to National Audit Office.

Well, in many cases, a progressive career in accountancy requires that you have sufficient work experience. If you need to gain UK work experience in accountancy, TD&A certified accountants may be able to help you. Visit their website at: http://tdanda.co.uk/careers/

Now having listed all of the above top 10 jobs you could choose as a career path in accounting, let's look at some of the key strategies and principles that can help you secure one of the above mentioned jobs.

The Top five things to do during an interview

If you are successful in a job application and you are called for an interview, here are top five things you should do during your interview:

- *Be honest – don't try to make up an answer if you don't know something.*
- *Show evidence of your competencies.*
- *Communicate clearly – eye contact, answering questions fully, using appropriate language are all important.*
- *Show passion for the company.*
- *Be professional.*

Besides knowing what you should do at interviews, you should also know what you should not do at interviews. Here they are:

- *Don't rush into giving an answer or response to a question, ensure you understand what's being asked and consider the context of the question.*
- *Do not go unprepared and make sure you have thought about the sort of questions you might be asked and have examples for each question.*
- *Refrain from using technical jargon where possible and talk about your contribution to a task, not just what your opinion or point of view on the subject.*

How to successfully manage your probation period

To make this book go that extra mile, I would like to talk briefly about how you can successfully manage your probation period after getting your ideal accounting job

The probationary period is designed to ensure that your colleagues support you and help you to make a smooth transition into working for and with them.

Your probationary period will also most likely be monitored by human resources department who will offer different contractual terms during this time. This may be in the form of a starting salary that will be raised on completion of the period. It will also usually involve a different length of notice period on both sides, meaning that if you wish to leave the job you have to give less notice than in your period of permanent employment, but equally your employer has to give less notice in order to end your employment.

The length of probationary period differs between organisation and jobs roles; in some places it can be as short as a few months, in others it can be several years. In most junior accounting roles it is about 3 months

It can feel at times as though you and your performance are being scrutinised with no benefit to you at all, but this is not the case.

This period provides a chance to find out whether the job is right for you: perhaps you will begin the job and really dislike it, or your personal circumstances will change.

The probationary period provides an easier 'get out clause' than your full time employment would. Also your department or team will offer you extra support to help you fit into the job, so take advantage of all that is on offer.

Some companies will provide you with a mentor who will be the first point of contact if you have any issues or uncertainties, and he or she will be available for informal meetings on a regular basis to check your progress and don't worry if you have no mentor, you will still be able to manage the probationary period well if you determine to.

So, how do you get to a flying start with your new employer during this probationary period?

Being an employer myself, here are some suggestions.

Let me first of all begin by saying that this is not the same as going for a promotion where you have to try to show that you are doing more than your current role entails and equally it is not like having an extended job interview.

No, none of those.

It is about impressing your employer & show them that they did the right thing by choosing to hire you over the other candidates.

So, here are some things that you can do to impress your employer during your probation. They are more like important indicators that your employer will be reviewing to assess whether you fit the role or not.

I will divide them into general and specific indicators.

Here are the general indicators your new employer might review.

i. Punctuality:

Punctuality is vital, as is attending meetings and taking a full part in the life of your team, department or company. Just as you managed your time well during your job search, you should even more so now. Show that you are an excellent time manager. That will really score you good points during your probation.

ii. Team player

If volunteers are sought for particular projects or responsibilities, show that you are willing to take part.

iii. Open minded

Make an effort to familiarise yourself with the new way of working and to try to do your job well. Be open to new and different ways of doing things and learning new methodologies and systems.

iv. Be sociable

On a social and personal level take an interest in your colleagues and try to learn how the dynamics of your new company work. Learn the culture, familiarise yourself with it and get on with it.

v. Conflict resolution

It is inevitable that sometimes, something or someone will "get to your nerves" and make you feel really uncomfortable and perhaps even annoyed. I want you to remember that, the way you deal with conflicts speaks volumes about your character than anything else and make no mistake, your employer will keenly be watching you on this one.

> "All our dreams can come true - if we have the courage to pursue them."
> **- Walt Disney**

Appendix 1:

- *Time usage assessment & planner*
- *Job success action planner*

Time Usage Assessment & Planner - TUAP

My prime goal is:_____

I am achieving this goal by: D A Y: D D / M M / Y Y Y Y at H H : M M

Time	My daily activities	Time Taken to do the activity in minutes	(%) Percentage time out (1440 minutes)
	1.		
	2.		
	3.		
	4.		
	5.		
	6.		
	7.		
	8.		
	9.		
	10.		
	11.		
	12.		
	13.		
	14.		
	15.		
	Total		

My top priority today is: _____

This is what I should be spending most of my time doing: _____

_____

JOB SUCCESS ACTION PLANNER

Name:	Week commencing:	DD/MM/YYYY
My ideal job title:	Proposed Start date:	DD/MM/YYYY

Top 3 goals for this week / Date this week to achieve the goals

1	DD/MM/YYYY
2	DD/MM/YYYY
3	DD/MM/YYYY

No.	Things to do this week	Mon	Tues	Wed	Thurs	Fri	Sat	Sun	Goal	Achived
1	Search & apply for jobs									
2	Read: Psycho-cybernetics by Maxwell Maltz for 15 minutes									
3	Phone call/meeting with mentor									
4	Meeting with a successful person									
5	Direct call/contact with employers									
6										
7										
8										
9										
10										

Successful people I am meeting this week

No	Name	Day	Time
1			
2			
3			

Job interviews booked for next week

No.	Agency/employer	Date	Time
1			
2			
3			

Moments of reflection

What are you grateful for this week:

If you were to start this week all over again, what one thing would you do differently:

Appendix 2:

- *Sample cover letter 1*
- *Sample cover letter 2*

Sample Cover letter 1:

Your Name & Address

Date

Contact person's name in the employer company

Employer address

Re: Accounts Assistant position at ABC Company

Dear Ms. /Mr. _____

I recently came across your job advertisement for an accounts assistant at ABC Company and read it with great interest, as I believe my skills and experience match your position perfectly, some of which are outlined below. I have a lot of experience using Sage 50 accounts as well as dealing with the payments and receipts and the bank reconciliation. I also have experience dealing with the trial balance and profit & loss.

Essential required functions	My matching skills
Sales and Purchase Ledger	• *Raising & posting invoices in a timely manner.* • *Obtain authorisation from the appropriate person for all purchase invoices & liaising with suppliers.* • *Process payment runs to suppliers based on invoices approved for payment prepared by the Financial Accountant and approved by the Finance Director.*
Monthly and Year-end Accounts	• *Preparing the monthly bank reconciliation, accruals & prepayments schedules for review by the Financial Accountant.*
Credit Control	• *Reviewing debtors & collecting outstanding debts* • *Carrying out credit checks on new clients*
Admin duties	• *Excellent telephone mannerism* • *Friendly & professional*

I would be honored to have the chance to further discuss your position as an accounts assistant and how my qualifications and background match the needs of ABC Company. Please contact me at 077123456789 or email candidate@yahoo.com.

Thank you for your time and consideration.

Respectfully,

Your name here

Enclosure

Sample Cover letter 2:

Your Name & Address

Date

Contact person's name in the employer company

Employer address

Re: Accounts Assistant position at ABC Company

Dear Ms. /Mr. _____

I recently came across your job advertisement for an accounts assistant at ABC Company and read it with great interest, as I believe my skills and experience match your position perfectly, some of which are outlined below.

I have a lot of experience using Sage 50 accounts as well as dealing with the payments and receipts and the bank reconciliation. I also have experience dealing with the trial balance and profit & loss & year end procedures

As you can see from my CV, I bring to the table X years of hands on professional experience including credit control where I have been able to successfully demonstrate competence in collecting over 85% of outstanding debts within weeks and improving the cash flow & liquidity position of the organisational. I also have experience dealing with HMRC, and liaising with both customers & suppliers in a professional manner.

I would be honoured to have the chance to further discuss your position as an accounts assistant and how my skills, competencies, qualifications and background match the needs of ABC Company. Please contact me at 077123456789 or my email address is candidate@yahoo.com.

Thank you for your time and consideration.

Respectfully,
Your name here

Enclosure: CV

QUICK ORDER FORM

Postal Orders

Sterling Libs Books,
Level 33, 25 Canada Square,
Canary Wharf London, E14 5LQ

Telephone Orders
020 7038 8370 / 079 7055 0865

Email Orders
handbooks@sterlinglibs.com

Please send me the following books, disks or reports.

TICK	BOOK TITLE	PRICE (£)
☐	Work Experience in Accountancy - Workbook	£45.95
☐	The Accounts Assistant Job Manual – How to do the regular day to day tasks of an accounts assistant in Sage 50.	£65.95
☐	Month-End Accounting procedures	£40.95
☐	The Trainee Accountant – How to have a successful accounting career	£24.95
☐	Get your VAT return done in 5 steps	£25.95
☐	Business Intelligence – Start, Build & Run your own business and become financially independent.	£20.95
☐	Management Accounting practical guide	£45.95
☐	The Way to Get an Accounting Job in the UK - The 5 strategic steps	£22.95

PLEASE SEND MORE INFORMATION ON:

☐ Speaking/Seminars & accounting job fairs   ☐ Consulting & mentoring

YOUR DETAILS – FOR US TO SEND YOU THE BOOK(S) YOU'VE ORDERED

Name:

Address:

City/Town: Postcode:

Contact No.:   Email:

POSTAGE & PACKAGING OF £5 APPLY IF WITHIN UK AND £9 FOR INTERNATIONAL ORDERS

QUICK ORDER FORM

Postal Orders

Sterling Libs Books,
Level 33, 25 Canada Square,
Canary Wharf London, E14 5LQ

Telephone Orders

020 7038 8370 / 079 7055 0865

Email Orders

handbooks@sterlinglibs.com

Please send me the following books, disks or reports.

TICK	BOOK TITLE	PRICE (£)
☐	Work Experience in Accountancy - Workbook	£45.95
☐	The Accounts Assistant Job Manual – How to do the regular day to day tasks of an accounts assistant in Sage 50.	£65.95
☐	Month-End Accounting procedures	£40.95
☐	The Trainee Accountant – How to have a successful accounting career	£24.95
☐	Get your VAT return done in 5 steps	£25.95
☐	Business Intelligence – Start, Build & Run your own business and become financially independent.	£20.95
☐	Management Accounting practical guide	£45.95
☐	The Way to Get an Accounting Job in the UK - The 5 strategic steps	£22.95

PLEASE SEND MORE INFORMATION ON:

☐ Speaking/Seminars & accounting job fairs   ☐ Consulting & mentoring

YOUR DETAILS – FOR US TO SEND YOU THE BOOK(S) YOU'VE ORDERED

Name:

Address:

City/Town: Postcode:

Contact No.:   Email:

POSTAGE & PACKAGING OF £5 APPLY IF WITHIN UK AND £9 FOR INTERNATIONAL ORDERS

"IF AT FIRST YOU DON'T SUCCEED, TRY, TRY AGAIN. Don't give up too easily; persistence pays off in the end".

–*Thomas H. Palmer (1782-1861)*

Printed in Great Britain
by Amazon